SELECTED POEMS

DOUGLAS FETHERLING

Selected Poems

ARSENAL PULP PRESS
Vancouver

For Val Ross
in friendship.

SELECTED POEMS

ARSENAL PULP PRESS
100-1062 Homer Street
Vancouver, B.C.
Canada V6B 2W9

The publisher gratefully acknowledges the assistance of the Canada Council and the Cultural Services Branch, B.C. Ministry of Small Business, Recreation and Culture.

Cover design: Gek-Bee Siow
Design & Composition: Vancouver Desktop Publishing Centre
Printed & Bound in Canada by Kromar Printing

CANADIAN CATALOGUING IN PUBLICATION DATA:
Fetherling, Douglas, 1949-
Selected poems
ISBN 1-55152-013-3
PS8561.E834A6 1994 C811'.54 C94-910726-3
PR9199.3.F47A6 1994

CONTENTS

Neon Autumn

Dubious Sunrise

Neon Autumn

PROLOGUE

When the heart skips a beat
the lights begin to falter in a show
of solidarity

This is not the apocalypse, it is
not even morning
                    but only a reminder
of what's obvious and basic:

We have forgotten nature so
nature, perhaps, has abandoned us

If this is the forest then we
must be the animals

WESTERN MANITOBA

For once the land equals the sky
in immensity, and the two work in conjunction
with the highway

we speed along, in disregard of haste,
since each mile is indivisible from the others
we leave each as we found it

only more so
We are safe now from oppressions
of the forest, where every night the ambushers

waited past their bedtime
We are tearing down the highway
and above us the clouds

are like opening titles of MGM's
most spectacular film
The sky in the west

grows progressively bluer, we are led
to expect some large celebration
when cement air and earth end together

in a point   Until then we are rotting
in speed less time and distance
two skeletons with maps in an old Chevrolet

DELIVER

Wet leaves don't crumble
and smoke doesn't make much of a shadow

on the night-lit asphalt floor

all these pieces fit together
now and I know

there are too many hours
but not enough time

to do anything that would matter

one used to be a better liar

ALLEYCAT

Simultaneous with this writing
the dull salutes of keys on paper
I live again
like an alleycat
silent on bricks and concrete
nimble on ledges and fire escapes
Back of the Yards
crossing the street
only when necessary
and then very quickly
head and tail
downward
the shortest path
between two points indistinct
in the night
then disappearing
into the shadows on the other side
seen for an instant under some arclamp
in the flashlight of some cop
or the headlight of a lonely car
no one knowing
whether it was me
or a crumpled piece of sports page
carried on a burst of wind
that seemed to come from nowhere

NOTATION #1

Above was a sign
which read in translation
Street of the Abortionists
where he was pulled
from his mother
                                        who had been
raped by all the races
with his eyes open
and his mouth
                                    in a high
and grotesque laugh
the doctor tried to silence
with a knife that came out
black

Born poor as well as naked
without money to bribe
or tip the executioner
he was his own mother
and like a seeing-eye dog
was never heard to speak

One eye was France
the other Japan
                                      and each day
he lived
someone else lived one day
less

Foetuses in amphorae
skeletons in cars

EXPERIMENTAL DEATH WISH 1927

Men in light-coloured suits
wearing flat straw hats called boaters
in England and skimmers in some
of the United States
jostle one another in the street below
looking and pointing at the man
on the ledge who jumps
that he might begin falling,
who plunges headfirst
towards a horizontal end
he knows to expect on the bottom again
if he rises too fast
and reaches the surface before the air
he expels

Each of the bubbles that float
in groups like bunches of grapes
about the diver's head
contains a suicide's modest donation
and will burst in the sunrays
on the roof of the sea
leaving it smooth the way an ash does
that falls from the cigarette
of a man in the crowd
to reveal the light intact
or disappears like the alcohol
of another stiff-hatted man
splashing and gurgling down the
flask's upended neck (bad booze
impatient to become bad urine)
or any of a thousand other similes

CAFÉ TERMINUS

The woman in red
with torch and flag
is leading us
                    someplace
off to one side
I cannot be seen
this is only the detail
of the picture

Her body is chunky
beneath the flowing dress
in this painter's style
hard nipples strain
representing art
and industry

The woman in red
but she's no lady
outside the theatre
Dillinger walking
missing the train where anarchy begins
at the turnstile
and the queue

And the dead stare out
from narrow coffins
appear to shrug
in the paper I buy
at breakfast
near the station
the pages turning brittle
as I read

ART ERA 1956

Terrible scenes
in parking lots
music like you
never heard
                    high above
on fire escapes
we dropped the empties
down the alley
the hits went ringing
into dented garbage cans
our misses struck
the pavement and opened up
like tulips

Days so bright
one could not sleep
nights condemned
as never long enough
we dwelt on them
like flies on sugar
too tired to say it
all again
               yet didactic
just the same:

foolishness
past such a point
is energy continued

We drank the drink
of whores
                 scotch & milk
or gin & Doctor Pepper
while I carried
your belongings
in a pasteboard valise

that was also desk
and pillow

We agreed
with our detractors
then went on working
as before
through eye level smoke
with a whisky belch
the stumbles and the shakes
                                                                at all times
avoiding progeny
as we now would avoid litigation:
stop it! I can sue you
for crying

report you
to the Ministry of Culture

POEM BEGINNING WITH A TITLE FROM PHILIP LAMANTIA

The ancients have returned among us:
at dusk the prairie wind is mixed

with old french strong as music
and heavier than air

Ancients follow seamless skies
to the distant imperfection

of shantytown
near the city's uncut ends

to visit those persisting
with traditions:

the hefty black revolver
that tattoo and that grin

OLD ELIJAH SPEAKING

I expected this face but did not predict it,
though there is a way of doing so I am afraid
I never learned:
like sawing a tree exactly parallel with earth
and knowing in advance the route of its collapse

Once the skin on my face was pulled down taut
and tied off at the chin like a sausage end,
but the years have twirled the knot loose
and let the flesh move upward, wrinkling this visage
that was smooth when we were young
My joints do not flex so unobtrusively as then
and recently cold objects have caused pain in my hands
and everyone seems older whom I met before today
and plans get less important but for time

I have lived in focus scarcely at all
for as a child I knew I was no child
as now I know I am not old

HARRY'S NEW YORK BAR IN PARIS

The bored waiter moves
towards you like a shark
in an aquarium
                    turning quickly
when very close
having lived here many years
he knows the limits
and where the glass is
and is able to seem
calmly efficient
                    while ignoring
the customers the dramaturges
who anoint themselves
                              and mumble
amen into their drinks
to combat power withdrawal

What you think is the mood
is really the smell
                      the threat
of posterity that keeps them
on their toes
                 all the colours
have to be imported
nightly smoke is flown in
                                special
like the noise
of the telephone ringing
with calls from persons long dead
and Jefferson's ghost
                           playing
the piano

TERATOLOGY

Tempo commodo

i.

His hair
rose up like splashed water
in the wind the train makes
leaving the tunnel
                                        confirming
an old suspicion that he was
meant to be drowned
discovered three days later
swollen and black
the gases released to float him
on the surface
of the cold mug of beer,
                                                    he complains
to the waiter
                                as the subway wheezes by
and the last car reveals him
the overhead lamps reflecting
on the spikes in the third rail
driven through his palms,
                                                    he awakes
in crucifixion
with a soreness in the throat
an ancient premonition of the gallows

Historically
only gentlemen
have died in bloodless profile;
the outlaw grows accustomed
                                                            to living
without future tenses
without benefit of cinema
he himself his only contemporary

a moth among dead flies
in the lightshade,
no longer able
to recall the days
he wanted to fuck the Matterhorn
and was perfectly willing
to allow the dew
on the grass in the park
to put a shine on his boots,
grows
accustomed to the days and years
he exists
without penetrating Future
careful not to return to the scene
of an error
his geography contracting
like a drying sponge
each night a deja-vu of the one before
every hour the place where the past ends
but the future never starts,
smoke
and a whisky chaser
for the former child in dead man's clothes
who has run out of trivia nostalgia
upset the balance of the ecology of time
and ends in the blue dark morning
in winter
knowing what it is that winos always mumble
lecturing on teratology to an audience
of cats
pissing on them
hoping it will freeze and render them immobile
but there is too much acid alcohol
his hands unsteady praying at his crotch
they show their teeth and spit,
when falling he tries to crush them
but they live to lick his face
hesitantly
like the first person to clap at the end

of a performance
he died while trying to remove his sins
stumbled and fell against the stone
there was no curtain call
                                        he heard
the terrible din of the subway wreck
lungs agurgle revolver poised
applause played backwards in a tape recorder

Stepitoso

ii.

One senses
old miracles when trying to knit
a grand tradition from common objects
not found in the home,
                                        one feels it
getting close or loud, sound or noise
music perhaps but mainly static
swelling into outrage
under the door
through the air duct,
                                    dropping notes
we open our mouths pressed against
the hole they slide our meals through,
someone happily pipes it in
joyously we inflate ourselves
float to the ceiling and burst against
the hot unshaded bulb
                                      Each morning
the keeper scrapes talent
off the walls sweeps up piles
of iconoclastic dust
puts us in a museum
we keep escaping from through tunnels
above which the street rings
hollow under boots

They lived against their better judgement
these men I am trying to return to
these elusive ones remembered
when I think beyond the laws
leaving messages
                                        with my finger
in refrigerator grease
so that health inspectors
of a later generation might
know that I have heard them,
the masochistic wisemen
the failed elite:
                                    Blake
madder than a hermit at the best
of times
                  Hearn poor man
one eye like a golf ball
the other just an empty hole
bumping into furniture in exile
spilling saki on himself
                                                De Quincey
we all know the story here
                                                      Machen
daft old Welshman growing nearer
and farther away,
things happen
in those hills
                                  Gourmont leper prince
keeping to his chamber
and Cendrars
                                   one arm to hail a taxi with
at Hollywood & Vine
                                               Bodenheim
with a three-day beard
and a bullet through his heart
                                                        Corvo
bitter little heretic
did your teeth smell bad

in the mornings
Huneker
were you right after all
Bierce
did you actually disappear
sliding down a bullet ridden wall
or open a lodge in the mountains
you and Traven
Saltus
were you as bad as you let on
Apollinaire
yes I think we agree the less said now the better
You should have seen Desnos
older than he should have been
at Buchenwald
cheering up the doomed
planning all the books he was going
to write
One liberator recognized him by his big dead sad
eyes
He had become a famous man
more an outlaw then than ever

iii.

They found him
in the alley in a see-through shroud
dead of multiple allusions
starved of his own traditions
by hearsay
innuendo
asphyxiated by everyone else's
replete with noise and implications:
the history of history
as told by survivors
who claim they thought it all
a good idea at the time
But in death
he was triumphant in his failure,

enemies gave up counting final scores
against him
god santa claus and the mounted police
stopped watching every move he made,
he frightened them in death as in life
he just annoyed them
                                        the clown and gipsy
the drunkard in the toilet
inserting his dime and sitting down
expecting to have his picture taken
angry and screaming later
using up all the soap
                                        pulling and pulling
the perpetual towel wanting to yank it
out by its roots like a flower
some pretty thing for which he has no use
(not the treadmill that it is)
and rising from the sink to the mirror
seeing himself the actual scholar
the prototype they had forgotten about
but still make money
showing movies of
                                    the cult of junkie
                                    the cult of loser
                                    the cult of saint
who on the negative genuflects backwards
speaks in asides but hears only language
stretched out to dullness
                                            a fortyfive
being played at thirtythree & a third
its tensile strength never tested
until it is too late,
                                    it snaps
and the body slackens
and the man within disappears
depending on how you look at it
taking failure to its true conclusion
by dragging it to the lowest plane

or failing still by having succeeded
in something at least
                                        with rookie cops
fruitlessly going through his pockets
and a man at the morgue on Lombard Street
washing his own trembling hands
                                                            in preparation
his face like that of an archaeologist
afraid of what he will discover

COMIC HOLY PICTURE: ECCE HOMO ONE MORE TIME

Tired bones
soak and go soft in his limbs
the noise of tiny erosions
keeping him awake
                                        on the bed
in a secondhand suit
intermittently abuzz with alcohol
and the free access
                                     of pain
like the orange neon gas
swirling in the heavy tubes
of the signs one never sees
any more
                    not flashing
and electric like the one
that goes
                 H
                     O
                         T
                             E
                                 L
                                    euphemistically
throbbing like his bloody fist
out of sync with the motion
of his lungs
                        and the squinting
which thought makes necessary now
that things are getting worse
not better
                    and two thieves
are snoring in the rooms
on either side

OUR MAN IN UTOPIA

The streets are so full of soldiers
one dare not risk drunkenness so often as at home

Instead, in fearful contemplation,
one keeps to one's rooms, which lighted
are no safer than the boulevards in darkness

The charges of the state's police
have in practice the force they lack in foundation

In the capital it is now a crime to be naked
and they say this is gaining favour
                                        in the provinces
as well

Yesterday some artisans were tried for being poor,
found guilty, their sentence kept a secret

For death, I have heard, people can be
posthumously indicted, the bodies disinterred
to lie before the judges whose faces
are hidden from no one knows whom

Statues of old heroes are replaced almost daily

The people of the street or rather of the shadows
don't know when to wave and cheer and when to look
away

Friends' salutations are guarded, the once-public buildings
patrolled

The price on my head is commensurate with
the value of truths I send by the bearer

CHRISTIE PITS IN AUTUMN

A mood like
that which follows
an argument, when

the two of you retire
to separate ends
of the apartment and

all sounds translate
as forensic devices:
doors gently

closed seem slammed,
words to the dog
are mutinous whispers,

each creaking floorboard
an insult by proxy.

Relations are touchy now.

There's a soreness in
the air, a question of
perspective

with the onion-domed church,
the line of big squat houses
(their anglos moved on long ago).

Some old quarries fill
with water, this one fills
with shadow.

BORDER CATECHISM

What is your destination?

Everyplace I go is Chinatown
these days when pandemonium need no longer
be a handicap and one puts up barriers
to keep out those who would erect
barriers against one

and otherwise makes do
with living best when cornered
surviving the cities, surviving the days
creating time by living through it
making it palatable, osterizing it
cleaning it up as a reformer would do
laundering it like a gangster his money
somehow, ultimately, pacifying the way

Tempus serva, mi fili reads
the inscription
Do so and the kindness is repaid

What is the nature of your visit?

To observe the passing seasons
on the ground and to study
geometry from above . . .

I want to see the city close up and how
it runs together in a kind of neon autumn
quiet optimism wrenched from bankruptcy sales
the miles of donut shops with karate schools upstairs
cinemas becoming bingo halls
when the people inside them
find their concentration waning

And yet I want to glide above it
for one never knows a city till one
learns it from the air
and sees how small it is and who
supports it with their lives
and what a struggle it is to linger
just a while longer in the clearing
when the forest is so near and the
aeroplanes overhead

Have you anything to declare?

Only that we're getting older faster now,
you and I, and that we can't go on
renegotiating the past like a mortgage
The terms are increasingly poor

There is little wisdom there for any
of us, we are fools to search out old comfort
like a picture of Christ hidden among the dots

You are a scapegrace (admit it)
as am I;
sophistication will not save us,
only compromise

I declare it is better if we're useful
I declare that it's best
to leave when possible
never having had your fingerprints taken

This is integrity
This is what innocence has come to

SUBROUTINE

One grows resigned
to living in a house where
pictures always need
straightening
and sleep comes on hot
nights thus:

a burial at sea;
the board is tilted and
one slips silently
below the surface where
noises though muted
stand out all the more

There are bottles
being smashed and Jamaican
imprecations and another
sound that could be weeping
but then again might be laughter too

and most especially the CPR heading eastward
as trains almost never do,
shaking bits of plaster
from the ceiling
raising puffs of dust
on the floor

Some night when we
have been properly conditioned
the bed may shake
though no train passes by
and telephone rings become
emphatic

until the morning when
we wake up
dead inside our clothes

Dubious Sunrise

ROUGH NIGHT AT THE HOTEL NONPAREIL

two a.m.

Our reputation has preceded us
up stairways and along corridors
which suggest now more than ever
the urine of persons long dead

We are going about our business
in streets of lost accents
and buildings admired
for their decrepitude
and as we do so we fail
to notice that our shadows
are of some different sex
some other form of mimicry
                                        entirely

There is a time and place for
everything and this is not the time:
for the fat man seated
in the phone booth staring outward
ever outward
                        nor the old guy
in the rocker eating a TV dinner
without teeth straight from the box
nor the night clerk with
the billy club hanging
behind the counter and the
expression of one who's learned
the hard way that retrospect
plays tricks

The city changes hands after dark
and by sunrise is entirely
given over to the few who've got away

They do not get misquoted
They do not get enumerated
They come at dawn to history;
it is like returning to the land

This is the parallel universe where
no one believes officials who
no longer believe in them—
who claim such persons are extinct
or if not why not?
that they're obsolete or some
trick of light

These people have been displaced
by theory which is a kind
of bloodless genocide

three-thirty-five a.m., in a storm

An individual in the act of
finding surcease in the storm

is illuminated

Each time the lightning comes
the city hides its shame
exposing everything else

The countryside worn out, ruined
just as these buildings are—
until at last the two
are in perfect balance,
the ego and the id
sharing a room together
to sleep and find
that dreams play tricks
                                        like people

There are mirages as solid
as the day they were built
and times when it doesn't matter
if the objects we heft and
show to best advantage in the light
will not in fact exist
when the darkness ends
We feel them while we have them
and this is enough:
we do not require museums

What do we need the
city for if not for this?
We are citizens or believe we are
with contacts, friends and the
power to ration ourselves
extend ourselves day after day
like exercise without the longterm
benefits

and we are right to do so
yet the facts escape or deceive us:
to this day no one knows
who assassinated whom or
where the wealth has gone
or why the best anyone can do
is to keep things in repair

Time doled out as talk and
sheets of paper
yet sometimes when you least
expect it
                  the truth shows through
like a dubious sunrise

This cannot be depended on to happen
and yet it is the only thing that works

four-ten a.m.

Supine on the hotel bed
the closed eyes see inward,
there are blue spots
turning yellow at the centre,
flowers becoming fireworks
through the magic of time-lapse
photography,
                                explosions in the
night like static electricity
followed by these brief
tremolos of pain

and this is about
as beautiful as it gets

No one wishes it so
but man in the end can only destroy:

What kind of refuge is this?
catching the bus after
the performance leaving the theatre
resigning yourself to
the absence of theatre here

everything at its most fragile
in the moment of silence
between applause and gossip,
the tail lights of the traffic
irradiate your going
like tracer fire,
every seventh bullet allowing a glimpse of what
you're trying to decreate

This is the way it is and
it's no one's fault we hope

Five-thirty-six a.m., near dawn

The ghost of the strongest
one I knew is in the dark
outside the hotel window

His discipline is still
the envy of us all
He made
a culture as he went along
carefully selecting from what
he studied and inserting
some additions of his own

He argued for need over desire
strove for thought over intuition
What he achieved was poverty
with none of its traditional rewards

Do not misunderstand:
this is not an easy one to eulogize:
he was a thief and a nuisance
who got on the nerves of
civilisation
yet his death was the film
breaking in the middle
of a boring movie it shocked them
to discover is reality after all

His colleagues spent their lives
as he did
practising emotions
which fail them now when needed;
they're angry still at being swindled,
they stare at one another
as the lights come up
whistling for the manager to protest
or implore;

each knows the secret none can prove,
the fact that he even
had secrets at all,
that it hurt when he concentrated
trying to be earnest,
that he was privately terrified
of most forms of power
and also of those who were not,
that the dark of the cinema
is really the light and that
all these condolences are lies

THE DARK GRID

In the cracks of this white city
there is another grid
                                        where applause
and politics do not exist
and politeness doesn't matter
You have seen me there
and know I know only the back doors
of restaurants
their distinctive arrays of garbage
little brick holes that are warm
for those not confused by purpose
a few spent aspirations maybe
but no purely theoretical contempt

Personally I no longer care
whether sleep is deserved or broken
by men at grimy loading docks
hurrying off into sunlight
                                                  No one
works for the government here
however indirectly
                                     no one has received
any mail in years
though you may write me if you wish
in care of the pigeons
                                          that waddle like cable cars
up steep tops of roofs
streetcars yclept desire

NOTATION #2

Ignorant child
                    playing
with a skull in its crib
has no sense of its unimportance
but pokes stubby fingers
through eye sockets
gurgling like a moron
takes a delicate cobweb
from the nasal cavity
                              twirls
it laughing around a finger
like spaghetti
                  (another tooth
drops from its place
in the jaw)

Neither does
the mindless infant comprehend
the symbol
               but rolls it
along the floor
it rolls fine on the cranium
but comes to rest on the horns
and neither do we
know the source of every dent
and trepanation
                      or the fact
that whoever he was was born
a skeleton and lived middle age
in an upstairs room
and laughed as he poured
the champagne on the roaches
that would not be drowned
that the yellow linoleum
was sticky for decades
                               past
old age and unto death

NOTATION #3

You are spilling out
through your pores
and onto the clean linoleum
What you are
has finally resolved itself
into its component elements
I hurriedly try to stop the flow
to mend the punctures
all over your body
In panic I stand your feet
in saucepans
It's no use
You empty while the room fills
Somehow I knew
I was born to be drowned
Artefacts and memories
bob on the surface

DEATHBED RAMBLINGS OF ANDREW HERON

Heron (1800-85) was the first white child born in York, now Toronto; in his middle years he operated a Lake Ontario ferry boat.

The irony is not that I was spared
the casualties of youth
only to be visited
by this disease;
the irony is that
I persist.

I shall die soon—
you may depend upon it!—
but I shall die not being certain
whether I am the last one remaining
who recollects the past
or believes it.

You ask about this place?
Indeed it was muddy as they say
but there was clarity.
Buildings were the proper size
for people, not for other buildings;
and such a man as kept a store
could talk with one that only
worked the land.
                                        Above all
there was joy in being young
when everything was young
but now the old has been replaced
and I alone survive.

You wish to have me
holding forth on great events?
I have told for years

how I was in Niagara Commons
the day the Yankees took
the town,
                    how even
at that distance
we heard the cannonade
and then the final rumble
which shook my elders
to commend the date
as one a lad should long remember.
And Mackenzie! yes!
a man of splendid maledictions
who scorned to look where
he planted them and suffered
no outrage but his own.
Or so I often heard it put
by others.

The shame is that History reposed
no confidence in such as me
till most of us were gone,
and now comes all this pother
about events I cannot recall
if indeed I ever noticed.

Those books they write!
Such conjecture!
                                That may well
have been what happened
but not how it felt to be.

History is not what occurred
but only what can be called back.
History is in the hands
of conspirators!
                              How Mackenzie
would have relished it
unless I miss my guess.

So I am the only one
to tell you how people walked
and what they used to say
and I am the only one to realize
that buildings have ghosts
like people.

Please do me the kindness
of a meet and simple funeral.

Let me be remembered
as a boatman
who measured time from one shore to the other.

INSCRIPTION FOR A CENOTAPH

Unable to speak, we were thoughtful
Blindness aided our concentration
The days had more effect on us
than we perhaps on them

We were brave, but in small doses
When dispossessed we prospered
and beaten for confessions
gave forth manifestos

Decay cured us of nostalgia
The noise became our friend

Do not gainsay us
We proved nothing
We lingered without waiting
and comprehend but cannot hear

NOTATION #4

If it bear fruit
the weed should offer no
affront to the gardener

But logic does violence
to passion, the weed
is random, it lives
off others, it spoils
the symmetry and the
fruit is bad

I am the weed
Thou art a flower
The scythe is sharp
on one side only

NOTATION #5

The ocean takes its roar away
leaves foam in your mouth
and salt in your dreams

The pain is there
but you don't feel it

Shards of glass like snowflakes
no two ever the same

THE IMPERIALISTS' ATTITUDE IN RESPECT OF THE TROPICS: PANAMA

Prior to decay there was life without culture
Time passed in fiscal years

Until the setting decomposed nicely
the people led lives of orthodox dread

(Mold proceeds in a slow spill up the walls
while new cracks appear and
others heal themselves)

The decay is a kind of pollution
but vitamin enriched; tasteless, odourless

We sip it with brandy in the courtyard
following a meal

Later as we perch on the old wooden gallery
it lingers above the rooftops like a halo
only shapeless

It's now in itself the principal export
chief industry, major resource

and part of our sorrow is that the sorrow's gone
leaving only tourists and derelicts behind

THE SIX O'CLOCK NEWS FROM BUFFALO

Once there
were streamers to greet
each famous visitor

these turned
to cobwebs
before they disappeared

and waterfalls
became escalators
which finally broke down

in the surefooted
progress of decay

with its gaudy colours
pinball lighting
and not unpleasant odour

that's carried across
the lake
with a faint suggestion
of all-time polka hits

Where are
the Natives of Cheektowaga
Tonawanda Lackawana
gone these two hundred years
nearly as extinct as the
foundry worker
the housewife in Depew
we're told of breathlessly
with mock grimness
as the music swells

Why is the politician outside
the courthouse hiding
behind his hat

who knocked over the
elemental liquor store

who set the fire
on Genesee Street
that burns oblivious

like
some eternal flame

CONTRIBUTOR'S NOTE

The author wishes to remain anonymous
The author is a figment of our collective imagination
The author is trying to get by in a world he never made
The author is a symptom
The author is a friend of the deceased
The author isn't bad just misunderstood
The author could not be reached for comment
The author is the pick of the litter

The author brought it on himself
The author is in capable hands
The author is responding well to treatment
The author is an open book
The author is a *cause célèbre*
The author is a victim of rising prices
The author is his own worst enemy
The author made it look like an accident
The author was arrested on suspicion and
died of complications

The author was a champion of the underdog
The author was out after curfew
The author was shaped by his environment
The author was old enough to be you equal
The author was in transit when the problem arose
The author was not to be trusted
The author was not to be fooled with
The author was mentioned in dispatches
The author was always in the line of fire

MOVING TOWARDS THE VERTICAL HORIZON

i.

A whistle blew and everyone still left
        was declared a winner
a whistle blew and everyone who had money
        was assured of being rich forever
a whistle blew and the moment was made
        permanent
through the entire known world it was
        the same and would forever remain so
no other landmarks than the ones already
        in existence
nor any other players
        statis everlasting, with nothing to
        wear out and be replaced and so
        no future, little past
from now on this is how life would be
A whistle blew and everyone still there
        was considered lucky at first
wherever you were when the whistle blew
        that was your own personal frontier and would
        have to be protected

Nothing is set down here but that which
        memory was holding
        the day the screen went down

ii.

Advice . . .

avoid the spotter planes by
whatever means you can

usually this requires moving
towards what's most remote
staying away from water
they follow rivers and then

the streams that give
themselves to rivers

there's said to be an
unspoken agreement
that they won't bother you
once you get the roof on
though they note
locations, coordinates
every winter they find
new ones, little smears
of smoke at right angles
to the cold horizon
it all goes in the database

we've been intercepting
your thoughts, have a file
this thick on your fantasies
you've been warned about
your dreams, your friends
are all deader than you are
we can identify your sources
and your benefactors
do not petition us for
justice
it would be too late
for that even if it weren't
an alien concept
be grateful we allow
you this last idea
then you begin serving
your sentence—
an eternity as smoke

Moral . . .

put the roof on first and
don't believe rumours

iii.

Once it's written down it's no longer true

When you create a file you are dealing
with stillborn information

Photographs have been worthless
since it became so easy to enhance them

When there is no means of giving proof
there is no reason for anyone to hide

Everybody stays silent

Not exactly what St Anthony had in mind

iv.

Christ was alive
one of only 300 million
when Natives met here
to trade and discarded
these broken tools
in what, then as now,
was alluvial mud

(each spring the stream
runs high and cold)

they didn't know of Him
nor He of them;

at Contact, say 1600, there were only 500 million
persons on the earth,
by 1750 still only 700 million
the aboriginals already proscribed
doomed;

by 2010 you will have your choice
of 35 cities with over 8 million
people apiece

the rich with concertina wire
and broken glass atop floodlit
garden walls,
the others in corrugated tin shacks
if they're lucky
if they're not among those
taken out by disease:

cities maybe but not metropolitan
for there is no polis
but a new distinction not yet
coined, only to be lost—
some other generation can
recover it

Look at your density map and see
where there are fewest, and go there

take up what was dropped as worthless

prove to these skeletons they were wrong

v.

I once thought I had
uses for novels that were
practically trash in 1910
and now are almost art
grammars of decaying languages
accounts in several volumes
of wars between those
who declined their nouns
and others who did not
books by explorers, works
of *philosophy* well disguised
ones that were in themselves

accomplishments
and earned their authors
obituaries in The Times with
remarks by ambivalent colleagues

I am selling them back to
second hand dealers who got them
second hand from their rivals
to and fro for decades
no one reading them but me perhaps
and with the money I shall buy
supplies, tools to make other tools
the types of food one passes
on to one's descendants
patches to repair anything
until the patches become the object
a means of escape, a method
of confusing anyone who follows
a different reality and
a different identity (both have
much to do with colour)
a revised and much improved past
as advertised
wholesale to the public
a poncho that's also a hammock
and doubles as a one-person tent

vi.

A monastery and a fortress
are very different places from
the outside

Inside one is apart from
that which one is a part of

Behold the similarity
and celebrate it

note the distinction
when you rub it out

vii.

Better when people needed only one name
even that a simple description
the fewer people the fewer names
several lives in which to say them

When the ground is warm you farm
when it cools you build and when the sun
presides you move and when night
interrupts you grow in the dark like a root

viii.

I know that like the last one
he would enjoy tracking me
down to some bare foreign room
demanding what was due years earlier;
therefore I wear gloves

indoors to prevent
fingerprints from adhering to knobs, window latches
I wear these gloves
making it hard to read
what's been written down
or to write more
the keys all feel the same
the skin all feels the same
when you wear gloves in riverine
operations they dry long
after you do
the leather shrinking
a minor spanish torture

I know there's some swelling
but can't see how much

torture is the waste-product
of government

ix.

The first job was to put up a cache
it is now a kind of lookout tower
the guard sits surrounded by
water-bottles from the dump
she watches for invasions, not homecomings
we are our own descendants
so auto-archaeologists as well

x.

The past is spent
the future lies in ruins
but is not a ruin
the debris is fertile
our escape a pilgrimage
this is what's important

Water that runs for five miles
over rock, mud and sand
has been returned
to original purity
but only if the stream
itself is clean

Q:
what if it flows through
a carcass just beyond
the reach of our senses
what then

A:
living downstream is always
an act of faith

xi.

No this is not some new fashion
it is the change of seasons
which is always and is never
obsolete

and one is both carpenter and cook
it is the same skill
one is better at it outdoors
reusing existing materials
where possible

(whoso would fear the young
does well to recall how two
old pints make a quart
assorted seasons a year)

There is no logic to
saving cut nails
but we do, in an earthen
jar dug up in the garden
they're shaped like teeth
iron teeth, were teeth once
a few more must lie
scattered around the
foundation under
a sprinkling of soil
exactly what archaeologists
expect to find
at gravesites

We agree that some
things are better inherited—
in the city, silver perhaps
but up here tools
prybars to pull apart
moaning boards
chisels and mortises
two saws and an axe

until finally it's time
to build not raze
chalk line, plumb bob, rule
appear to measure the
performance
hammers in the hand
attack the nails like
hummingbirds

(the seasons have revolved
once more, it is
spring now strange to say)

xii.

This is what keeps recurring
that in the past
one could not possibly
have known, that now
it is too late, that by
taking time to consider this
one loses the
last opportunity

such is one way history
piles up; there are
others

Fools argue but we
invent the past more
than we control
the future
use the present to merge
dreams and likes
catoptric recollections
into something that
is safe, anonymous
we can taste it
whenever we wish

xiii.

A makeshift bestiary. . .

observe the insects
and how they come when
the sun goes down
(artificial light would
not fool them)
making their way across
the floor, into the basin
out again around
any object they choose
not to conquer
for reasons of their own
they know their limitations
they feel their way along
they are cautionary tales

The dog is the noblest
creature here today—
natural philosopher
uninterested in material
things, extending trust
before receiving anything
at all, always in accord
with wherever she lies
a natural physician too
though the stretches that
look like exercise
are actually daily prayers
violent ones followed
by complete rest
alternating through the day
like many small meals
in the place of one large
and unlike the squirrel
that's briefly still
but never idle
the horse that contemplates

so much that patience
has ceased to be a virtue
but our model should be the cat

Cats never give their
right names

xiii.

This is the way wars began
wars began wars began
with diners intimidating
foreign-looking waiters
and some ass saying it
would all be done
by Christmas
                as the Press
reported on good authority
how the enemy were hoisting
infants on their bayonets
far away

later, when the proper
side had won, survivors
would go to barbershops
and reminisce without
talking without
intending to

there were certain
procedures to follow

being premeditated
events were predictable
to someone

there was order if
not accountability,
people lost their lives
and missed the party

but at no time did anyone
discover he was melting

xv.

Each generation believed itself
a moral and cultural advance,
that was the secret where the poison
was hidden
that was the key to organized decay,
playing on fear, stupidity
the predictability of it all
promoting decline from fashion
as a kind of fall from grace
the slipping away of timeliness
much as the spirit fades
or the body dies

The guilt of not being there
was the guilt of generations,
a terrible thing, fearful
the way it was ascribed and bartered,
one grew older without wisdom
painful associations relived
none but genuine guilt accepted here
buy one get one free
it was a strictly commercial proposition
that only the trivial took seriously

Resistance begins with the will to resist
resistance and acceptance the magnetic tension
resistance the better part of growth

Towards the end there were too many
images, too many sounds, even more music
than one could tolerate
too much of what passed by distracted
us from knowing any of it well

So what we couldn't carry we left to rot
what was not examined, wasted
now we make whatever we require
never wish for more than we need
never hope for less than we deserve
surplus and sufficiency
equals darkness plus noon

xvi.

Those which never worked well anyway
they were the first to collapse
laundromats were among the earliest
buildings to be used for shelter
the newly homeless drove out the derelicts
then were driven out themselves
when the shit became too deep in the corners

curiously, the post office still processed
the mail long after there was anyone
to take it to its destination
one sometimes came upon huge bundles
of it in the streets
one night I saw someone burning it
in a trash can, someone who still had matches

It wasn't long before you got to the point
of not knowing anyone listed in the phone book

in a world without order, this was freedom

xvii.

If you don't have possessions
then you don't have to break as they do
though you still make choices
this is one of the rules so easy
to remember

do you pick an eminence
that defends itself and rely
on cisterns
or remain in the valley
water's flowing there
but high ground on two sides?

Flight is no escape from compromise
but a journey to find the primitives
they had good reasons for
believing as they did

Build small and build thick
several locations
a day's patrol between them
better than one big one
surrounded and surprised

There's still much to be said
for the square two-storey box
without doors or windows below
just a ladder someone lets down
or you pull up behind you
there's life in old ideas yet

The separate kitchen reduces danger
build it plumb and secure it
find the old dump now buried
for bottles broken ones

can be cut down later with ice
from the lake and fire from the sky
but use little that was made by man
no plastics, rubber, aluminium

Your best protection once
was anonymity; that didn't work
now the plan must be to
rearrange what nature gives you

a field strewn with rock is a wall
that awaits assembly
not like the city where all was
allegory, sex a metaphor
respiration syntax

Everything was a symbol then
now everything's a kit

xviii.

There's no place you can go
where the art police won't search

no place you can go that others
haven't given up on
choose one and dig in
find one where the undergrowth
is returning and the camouflage
agrees with your complexion
locate the point at which
tyre tracks and bear tracks
look the same, not two lines
moving in opposite directions
but one line, a vertical horizon
and once you're there do
whatever you feel you must

defend the perimeter if you like
make your trenches zigzag
put grenade sumps inside,
the command post well back of course
its roof the strongest plane
lay down burster material
to minimize the scatter, dig
a bloody moat if you have to
follow the rules

what's fixed cannot be moved
and is subject to infiltration
never allow blind spots
to develop in your field of fire
cut down possible losses by
dispersing anything of value
remember, in every conceivable situation
it's better to wait for darkness
and so on, folk wisdom for the times

If you do the job well
the art police won't find you

xix.

Overheard . . .

let us rejoice in the enemy, the other side
not individuals but an enemy caste
born to be somebody's enemy, bred for it
as others think they're bred to lead
they've become accustomed to that for
which they were reared
their destiny fulfilled by your hatred of them
the unrelenting sameness a part of
the sentence they serve

there's too little praise for that which
is beautiful, none at all
for such a beautiful enemy, splendiferous
in their isolation and inescapable defeat
save in that which makes them so invincible

there are not ideologically correct
they never know how much they weigh
television cannot touch them
they are worthy to be our enemy

xx.

Nocturnal triads . . .

Foil sabre epee
strophe antistrophe epode
endless triptych panels
whose medium is shadow
whose message is always
to communicate best
one had best use rumour
and the occasional aside

Use stone to keep down weeds
letters to keep down calls
the telephone to keep down visits
everything is prophylactic
still nature reasserts itself
the elemental things returning
in novel combinations

Paper covers rock
scissors cut paper
rock breaks scissors
rock breaks shovel
rock tries patience
rock makes days so difficult
rock keeps us humble and productive
rock speaks for itself
once the facts have been established

Scissors cut along dotted line
scissors like surgical instruments
scissors originally seemed destined
for something better than this

Paper an affront to rock
paper gives scissors a reason to exist
paper ignites, consumes itself
yet paper keeps the lasting record

immortalizes rock, is granted
immunity from scissors

MasterCard beats Visa
American Express beats MasterCard
that which we wish to forget
that which we wish to remember
accumulate together, indivisibly
the good and the bad the only real surprises
one phone leaves its number for another
the pressure always mounting
there is too much precision
for this to be coincidence
again and again, on and on
endlessly in the preternatural quiet

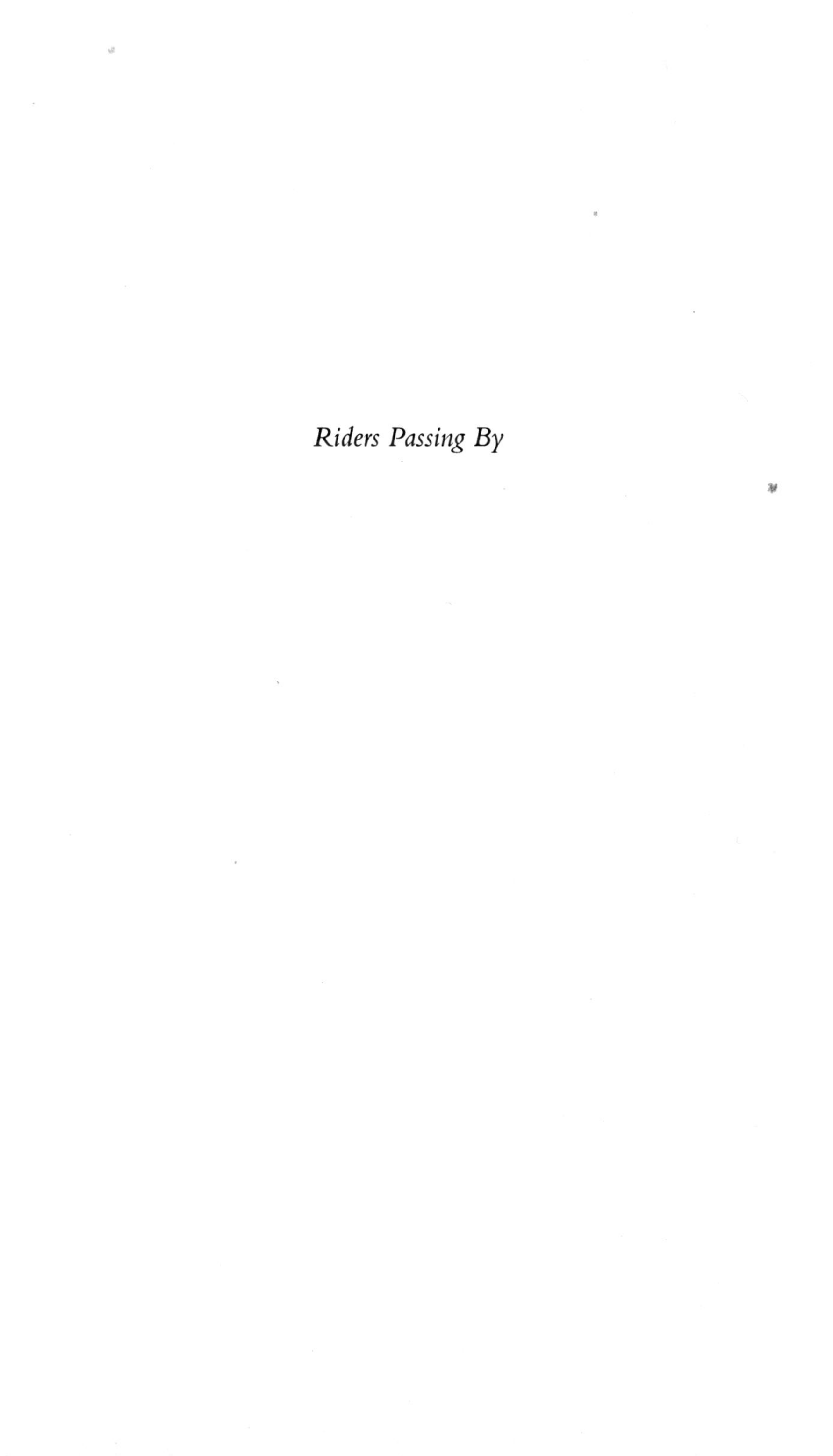

Riders Passing By

RITES OF ALIENATION

i.

Dead street late at night
even the homeless gone home
a blind man's cane protruding from the rubbish

ii.

Car park attendant
in lonely hut with saxophone
an audience of empty Buicks

iii.

Let the record show
that details are lacking—
bogus dawn hesitates over rooftops

iv.

Alms from heaven
night-birds strike the CN Tower
breakfast for the derelicts

v.

The present is blocking the future
southbound towards delusion
seven a.m. on the Don Valley Parkway

vi.

Bits of old messages
in layers on the answering machine
a bristle from the brush embedded in the portrait

vii.

Old man sitting in the park
grey pullover keeps out autumn
the last leaf remaining on the tree

viii.

Two joggers in the rain
a red-haired woman reading Aldous Huxley
—not much to show for a day's work

ix.

Conscience and indigestion
danger increases as the seasons change
utopia made her claustrophobic

x.

Petroglyphs sprayed in alleys
but invocations go unanswered
the innocent traveller steps from the kerb

xi.

Big greasy snowflakes
plunging to the street outside
the waitress 10 years older than she was 6 weeks ago

xii.

Tomorrow's archaeology today
the mirror's backed up again
office towers sweating

xiii.

Main title theme & incidental music
the waitress is really an actress
tips & applause

xiiii.

The walls inhale
thinking of Byzantium
seven passengers arise

xv.

He answered the door once too often
got nailed
three days later resurrection

xvi.

"The city is something you do with space" *(Thos Merton)*
buildings bend before they break
sway in time with the silence

xvii.

The world is too much with us
we have given our hearts away
says the man taking notes at the party

xviii.

Language derives from sighs
bills of atonement
the past is legally binding

xix.

Buzzards stake out those
who circle in four-door sedans;
two weeks of expressionist rain

xx.

The after-hours joint
where all the bartenders hang out
the animals' field-trip to the zoo

xxi.

Quiet the streetcars sleep here
fresh snow a security device
predators trapped in deafness

xxii.

Old wallpaper
down down, layer after layer
each one nearer the truth

xxiii.

Rain will wash away
what the windows have seen—
the image heals itself

xxiiii.

Language has been compromised
the evidence points to us
we reinvent ourselves once more

xxv.

Memory lapses, distortion, evasion
nobody knows who owned it first
their lifestory grew like a folksong

xxvi.

Blackmail often found in nature
the wind goes unreported
snows muffle

xxvii.

A crooked face in the mirror
rewrites itself—
truth concave, never convex

xxviii.

Undocumented language
impossible to trace it
the less said now the better

xxviiii.

Return journeys always lighter
we choke on tears
leaving stains instead of shadows

xxx.

Nightwear nightware nightmare nightmirror
we're locked in these conspiracies together
a kind of black communion

xxxi.

The hare pulls back from the wolf
horizon receding as we approach it
ambush a possibility

xxxii.

Nightshade nightshape nightweight nightscrape
rust the strongest bond all right
but which is the strictest emotion?

xxxiii.

Neither proof nor cover-up
conspirators can be victims too
not implicated in anybody's dreams

xxxiiii.

Memories command a premium
the transcript proves it
but I digress

xxxv.

The night continues to expand
somewhere dogs ask questions
for sirens to answer

xxxvi.

Are we rushing or escaping?
elderly nomenclature
does not keep the hunter humble

xxxvii.

Master does well to emulate dog
stop breathing every few seconds
listen hard for enemies

xxxviii.

Too many secrets swallowed dry
new shoes squeak underfoot
branches moan in the wind aloft

xxxix.

Three men wearing silhouettes
hazy figures on a railway trestle
my lawyer advises me to write no more today

xl.

The land is mostly water
the contest lasts for aeons
floods keep score

xli.

Trust the road to remain beneath us
reckless in blue-black night
frantic for a destination

xlii.

Salvation
light in farmhouse window
like warm yellow cheese

xliii.

The clouds withdraw
dragging their wounded shadows
across the field to safety

xliiii.

An arrow to indicate the Fraser
thin line of buildings
near the canyon floor

xlv.

The continent ends in exhaustion
timid waves a form of welcome
you coin the term British Columbia

xlvi.

The ocean snores and wheezes
hands of the clock like an insect's feelers
desperately seeking the past

xlvii.

People at the aeroport
dragging bags pets children
only the bags are on wheels

xlviii.

Spring is our manumission
perfection we rejoice in
then the cat eats a butterfly

xlviiii.

Staring the way a lip-reader does
at the jukebox of dreams
unable to decide

l.

To live longer is to concentrate
on speed devoid of motion;
wait for riders passing by

li.

Who picks the ending supplies the meaning
words in clusters not regular breaths
conversation has ceased being oral

lii.

The prisoner ties blankets together
like St John of the Cross (or Jimmy Cagney)
ivy up the barbed wire creeps

liii.

The flame stumbles then rights itself
with opening and closing of the door
deliveries : departures

liiii.

Tears from beneath the blindfold
just think about them and snap they're gone
the blindfold is a kindness really

lv.

Everything was obvious in context
a bottle of blended
a distinguished air

lvi.

Knocking at the gate in code
speaking fluent gibberish
less civilisation than is called for

lvii.

Faint carbon paper tattoo
image slips away like a dream
objects leaving unclaimed stories behind

lviii.

Entire new season of desires
hidden among the effects
countervailing shadows

lviiii.

Starting a new list
rescue paraphernalia
untranslatable scrawls

lx.

Retroactive silence
the saxophone expunged
our feet create erasures

lxi.

The night falters
moving towards repose
harmony with a bit of kick

lxii.

Shadows crosshatched
dark to light
the sun erases

lxiii.

Inviting confusion
the ratio of dead to living
plugs began falling from their sockets

lxiiii.

Our faults do not redeem us
we're disposed of when we're gone
lightbulb no substitute for fire

lxv.

In wind or underwater makes no difference
elements are there to grind you down
the I of the poem, the you of the song

lxvi.

Read on
ransacking shelves
the dead leave messages in books

lxvii.

The moon's brown nipples—
every object in the room
emitting a metallic buzz

lxviii.

Positive ID
tattoos shaped like stains
appear then disappear

lxviiii.

Progress towards decay
it just got away from us somehow
the city sprung

lxx.

Unwelcome reminders of the dead
not facts you can look up
astringent through the would healed long ago

lxxi.

Bad storm brewing
neatly xeroxed leaves
torn from trees

lxxii.

Height precedes width
etiquette demands it
organic forces exerting control

lxxiii.

Branches thick on the ground
nostalgia for the storm absolute
reminiscent thunder

lxxiiii.

We vary our routine
the enemy are reptiles
never wear the same skin twice

lxxv.

Hermit with no hermitage
stands firm on paradox
a name is still required

lxxvi.

Art flourishes in strange precincts
life drawing offered at the morgue
books written at the university

lxxvii.

Not the poet but her poem
not the image but the sight
the process lived, not the act observed

lxxviii.

One cannot rest
in one's own shadow—
seek the shade of friends

lxxix.

Self-educated
never had a lesson in our lives
no one to share the blame

lxxx.

Old movies:
the dead cavort on screen
the reel unwinds

lxxxi.

The rain searches everywhere
we hold our breath
act nonchalant

lxxxii.

Disappeared
while on retreat
lapsed into exile like a coma

lxxxiii.

High notes piercing the wall—
visible through the window
a plastic moon with cigarette burns

lxxxiiii.

What's left nourishes
make sure it's someone else's
we misjudge our own nostalgia

lxxxv.

We know at all times where our shadows are
but are we inconspicuous
in the desert?

lxxxvi.

Self-destructive behaviour
if you want it done right
do it yourself

lxxxvii.

A little place in Zen Street
buttons on the mattress, life goes on
the blood has settled in the roof of your mouth

lxxxviii.

In hot countries near the floor
we stand erect as bad air rises
jaywalking a western crime

ixc.

The future is forewarned
lying heavily upon the shelves
a trace of history around the rim

ixci.

Typhoon forecast
wisteria
hysterical

ixcii.

88 keys
37 buddhas
14 names for despair

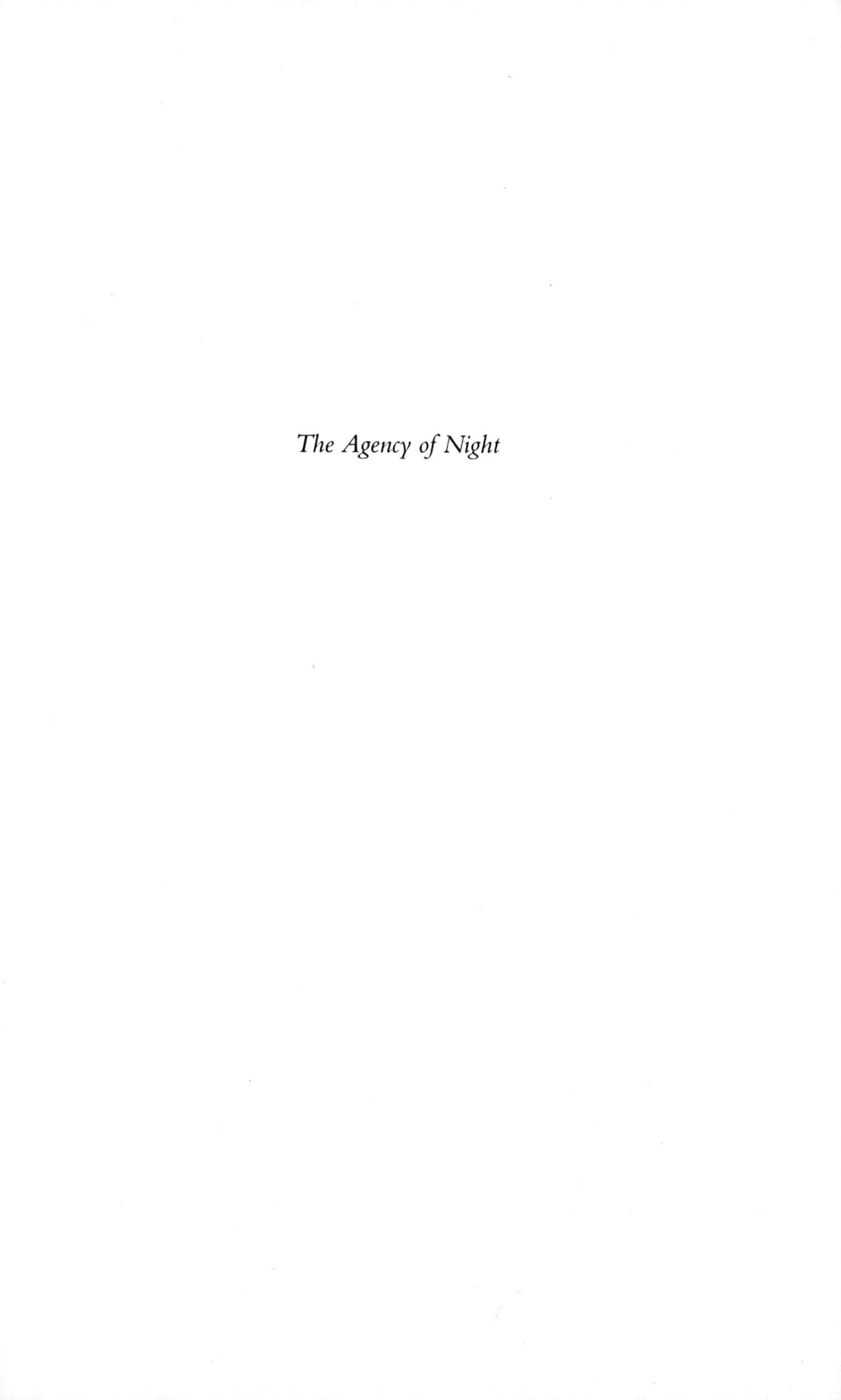

The Agency of Night

SUDDEN HARMONY

No incipience
but a sudden harmony.

Two figures in a
landscape
in a picture from
a text.

It's difficult
to choose the horizon
from among so many
planes.

The line ends at the point
where motion is set to
start.

Like a creature
hearing movement in
the underbrush
one waits in the rain
for the subtle change
in pitch.

Then the tide plays
arpeggios up and
down the beach.

FORENSICS

i.

Every act that
begins in homage
ends as surveillance.
Wires so thin we
pass through them
as the bass notes rise
through the floorboards
and the treble
penetrates the walls.

ii.

The past has gone dark
silence is the residue.
The memorials we make
forecast an echo.
We don't know where our joy
might lead.

iii.

A skyline of clouds
like a movie street
nothing behind it.

iv.

The tide is a drumroll
in a nightclub.

v.

It's only as fragile
as we permit.
Things we didn't know
had skins have them
after all.

Everything leaves traces
of its essence on
whatever it touches.
This is the secret
of human relations
and of scientific police work.

MEMORANDUM FOR THE FILE

i.

The sky all stained again

where the narrative leaves a trail
active but reactive also
and a shared chronology

for this is reputedly
the offspring of
another such day long ago

when morning was finally revealed
once silence reached a
crisis then broke like fever.

ii.

Waking up, moving out
from within, an attempt
at gesture

the anonymity that
lies behind the name
and discourses most sincerely
on its meaning.

In reviewing the life we review
the method.

In souvenir of the occasion
we set down these lines.

DISSIMULATION

i.

Going back under means
not being present any longer
where the only environment
is the threat of surprise;
the best companions are
those who do not follow.

A storm is driving us in
upon ourselves, we pile up on the rocks.
Particular cults grow reassertive,
friendship is sacrificed to a secret
support group, its members unknown
to one another.
They recall sensations they've had.

Voices without shading
narrate the event, administer the text,
the reading of which is like
the reading of a will, with the relatives
forgathered expectantly.
We have come to ventilate the
circumstances.

This is not an instance
of existing somewhere else
but an actual theory of absence
put into practice for effect.

Event is the term we use for episodes
we know aren't accidental.

ii.

We cannot habituate
ourselves to the rich
motive of opportunity
in the endings we enact.

Some wait for a sign
others watch for a signal,
some shadows are warm
others cold.

iii.

The words disappear
by falling into the page
a line at a time
like shooting gallery targets
on an endless belt.
They leave few ghosts
of their meaning.
So too are certain facts
consumed in the fibres
of the testimony heard today.
The burden of proof
lies with the weary,
the burden of recollection
also.

iv.

Memory with a half-life
of twenty-five years
quoted in the interior
in silence no doubt.

Let us not anticipate
its future nor regret,
let us mourn in our new
urgent grammar.

Absent some reason to
the contrary,
nostalgia will always
result in inflation.
So inveigh against
the past with its dubiety
and leverage.
Such methods are essential
for our sustenation.

v.

Of process.

The operative word is silence.

The paper grows foxed and brittle
and the past defines the content.

Days descend to us through the agency
of night, brightness decays into darkness
the constant breaking down of matter
and of data. The accountants
report a discrepancy
between yesterday and today.

We're left confused
by ambiguous sunsets, vague promises,
obscure indications of rebirth.
Sofar as one can descry
everything converges
through a tunnel towards a moment—
that is, if the truth can be believed.

vi.

The record is forever clear.

There's a waterfall in hell
where suicides never land,
a hotel in Vancouver with Niagara
two storeys high,
an excited crowd below
when the sign breaks open
and the life spills out.

Sparks like snowflakes
dying as they strike the pavement,
the mock hissing death of a
Chinese dragon but the writhing
wires are real.

PRE TEXTS

i.

Whatever we notice becomes
the landscape that documents itself

random cows graze beneath hydro pylons

white squares stiff on somebody's clothesline
except in propaganda a sight that's been obsolete for years

people in their living rooms living

a lone oak on a hilltop like a logo
a willow like an afghan hound

the Canada of the TV station sign-off
when ocean and anthem swell in agreement.

ii.

Anthropologists invaded once
the explorers' dirty work was done

same process, different perplexities

our best course now is confronting recollection
learning how circumstance favours the
higher elevations, how disputes are resolved
by the nature of things.

iii.

Irritating rain
like scratches on a classic film

ends, and a loon in the swamp bestirs itself
to recross the old denim sky.

RADIO

They enter by one earphone and
leave by the other: ghost narrations.
The sound of rats or someone trying the doorknob
(I don't mean the cop on the beat)
static like the table-talk of parrots
or scarlet monkeys screeching in trees
until a voice, maybe human, speaks
but hesitates, caught for an instant
before being sucked into the blackness
like a book thrown from the window
of a train (the pages beat as quickly
as the wings of a bird that senses
some danger unheard on radio
then dies).

This is what we use now in lieu of maps.
What comes to us is where we go.
Much depends on conditions.
Jailer, I insist on an omen to subdue
my doubts or, failing that, a radio.

I hear too many nasal accents,
see too many vacancies and embalmed businesses
and railyards where the only sound of life
is freight trains having rusty sex, yawning
and stretching in the distance, running
headlong at each other like whales
(they covet our stability, we envy
them their freedom).

Up all night with the fear of death
and the radio, listening in the dark
with middle-aged wonder
reminded of the old unbearable melancholy

made worse when there was nobody
to share it (or confide it to).

My dead friends
why can't I find you on the radio?

SPIRIT NOISE

The usages argue
that the function of the dead
is largely referential.

The way trees rise beside a stream
is how this town must have sought
the railway:

several houses, a stable, a store,
a building that can only have been
a hotel once

arranged on a road like the alibi
that a raindrop makes, sliding down
the window pane.

The echo speaks to us
from direct witness,
with memories of caesarean sunrise
and mornings so cold that
the locomotive saw its breath
as it snorted impatiently
at disestablished horses.

Such odd sounds, mere scribbles
on the air.

ANCIENT BELIEFS

Here we do
not worship ancestors
we treat them

for what they are,
part memory, part
parasitic affliction.

As one cannot prevent
them, neither can one
be completely cured
of other personalities
which persist inside our own.

Specifically,
we believe each of us
to be a pool
into which two streams empty
acid and alkaline
father and mother;
it doesn't matter which
is which, only
that there be two

recombinant, variform
fainter as we grow fainter
on the one hand Simulacrum
Recrudescence on
the other—
impressions of people
who bequeathed us all
the unused portions
of themselves.

It is also our belief
that what's not paradox
is allegory.

CARTOGRAPHY

How firm the curve
of the only coastline
how dark with our confidence.

A map is no journey after all
but a drawing, not holy
nor predestined, certainly
not true.

The beach lightly shaded
a trick of the pencil
extending no farther
than the highest known peak
in the nearest range of mountains
(crosshatching
to indicate farmland
comes much later if at all).

Beyond that only white
space unexamined, unexplained.

Exploration is the art
of the plausible so be free
with specifics.

There's room for a fancy
cartouche if you wish,
doodles in the terrifying
margin where saurian monsters lurk
(fugitives are genuine explorers,
all others parasites on the body
of invention).

The various shapes will have
colours assigned them,
but you know how the light
regards decisions.

Afternoon spills shadow
over the surface; it dries
to a rubbery texture;
in the morning, the sun
peels it back like a layer
of skin.

Each day you're surprised
how new the surface is,
how vulnerable
like a face.

ACCUMULATED WISDOM

An egg with two yolks means double the fortune
when you dream about eggs your health will be broken
when you dream about money your luck will desert you
when there's blood on your palm you will soon know
wealth
when there's blood on the moon the soldiers are coming.

To wear the shoes of a dead man is unlucky
a dead man's tooth carried in the pocket
is often proof against plague
earth from China will deter unwanted visitors
earth mixed with ashes from a fire caused by lightning
is the best defence against nightmare
there is no defence when the nightmares are real.

The child born on Sunday shall never be hanged
the child with a caul shall not drown at sea
the child bathed in brine will always be strong
the child who grows up shall remember.

TELEGRAPHIC INSTRUCTIONS

For art's sake look out
stop regard the threat
of rain that hangs
in a discoloured sky
observe how blood
adds flavour
to the pavement
how the gutters
fill with rubbish
how old sensations
still obtain.

Stop and take under advisement
this entire sad heritage of dreams

find some interior
means of becoming
the instrument we seek.

Wake up praying and
recall the limbs of trees
motioning through the glass
once silence became obsessive:

a hole opened up in
the darkness on this
very spot

remember?

FAINT BLUE WASH OF MOUNTAINS

Other cities exist because
of assets first exploited
then outgrown (rivers/harbours)
the sole advantage of this place
is climate it will never deserve;
skies too clear to be genuine
or for anybody to be useful
perfection leads to stupor, stupor to decay
hawked in the streets like bad food
pastels growing paler until they vanish
though always in the distance the faint
blue wash of mountains.

Mountains/city   city/mountains
this eye sees it one way and that another
neither is correct of course
always someone out of focus,
and now the picture's breaking up
images revert to dots.

TRAVELLING BY BUS (THINKING OF JACK BUSH)

The lost highway is in
good repair, but all around it
nature has died.
It has rained and there are
puddles in the underpass
though the rust with which
the hills are streaked
remains the best proof
of life.
It flows miraculously from
some holy wound.
The spectacle attracts no pilgrims.

Which should one follow when
history intersects the science
of it all?
                    Green bottleglass streams
dark clouds
                              some ancient source of regret.

So does the surface work its hardship
on us. There are no reminders
only shocks, however soft,
and a deeper order of things
lurking in the shapes
swimming in blues and lying
in reds, returning in the end
to ochre as all things must:
brittle and innocent near the rim
but the centre creamy and fertile.

BEGINNING WITH NORTH

First comes a white frame
house, ancient and decrepit
dignity wearing thin but upright
amid green hills and stooped shoulders
built by someone with the grit
of summer on the back of his neck
more comfortable designing barns perhaps
but all sorts of chores in a lifetime
rough stone foundation, strong
upright skeleton and plain facade
an arrangement of perpendiculars
on a curved background, white
slats against green foliage
overhanging the dirty river;
it's the custom to paint only
one side each year
beginning with north, the hardest
a small job never finished
always a contest between owner and nature
to see who gives up first.

—near Fredericton

APOSIOPESIS

i.

The fatal ligature takes its rise
from a feeling you once had

the experts all pronounce
in favour of its value

but to revisit the question now means
enquiring after the state of something

over which you have no veto.

ii.

Surveillance has only made the truth
more obvious—

unless it's scorched by recognition
nothing this important is ever said out loud.

iii.

When we were born, this dilemma was born alongside us
one of those accidents of culture

invoked in the language of extreme contrition
then urgently ingested

a secret that transpired despite our best efforts
a vapour that exceeded its ability

and vanished in a Javanese nightmare.

iv.

The entire legacy was a misunderstanding, of course
a bottle deprived of its contents, round end foremost

a false innocence no one believed
the blood like luxuriant draperies

data hunger breeds data sickness.

v.

In the circumstances, a diminishing response
seemed best

the silence intensified
we said it with ellipses . . . .

Do You Still See China When You Dream?

THE VIEW KEEPS REMINDING US OF FLAGS

The view keeps reminding us of flags
we don't wish to be reminded of
certainly not now, certainly not these.

Red in the morning, sailors take warning
but do they listen? Never.

Looking northward they sense freedom
where the rest of us can only prophesy.

Boats nervous at their moorings
the wind kicks up, the last ferry
waddles across the harbour.
The lights which struggle to stay visible
grow weaker all the same.
It's like something out of Bulfinch.
This ferry only goes one way!
And where exactly does that leave
the living? Exactly.

The eye of the storm, the eye
of the beholder of the storm: streaks
unfurl across the sky where someone
has pinned up a secondhand moon
like a lost object hanging
in the laundromat unclaimed.

WITH THE NAME GOES GREAT RESPONSIBILITY

i.

Be impatient with the device.
That's what I tell the young people.

The sources are hidden deep within
beyond the fingers of appetite
wrapped in a terrifying envelope
invisibly encoded.

Silence is not just the motto here,
it's the theme of our praise.
Clenched lips betoken honour
remote from the boundaries of response
beneath the awareness of sound
below the enemy's radar.

ii.

The name is ritual and if
it involves some destruction
they're sorry it cannot be helped.

The name is synonymous
with the death of landscape.
There's not even industry with
which to commune, only danger
minus relief or exhilaration.

When you speak the name
you spit poison in highly concentrated form.
With the name goes great responsibility
and even greater fear.
It's tainted don't mouth it
or answer to it.

You're guilty of uttering
when you say it out loud,
manslaughter when you linger
over the intent.

SIGNALS FROM THE CENTRE

Forgive such long silences
they come with irrelevance;
the doubt must run its course.

Admit a stranger
who saw your fire from a distance
but didn't know how to read it
so bright it seemed
against the blue-black sky
when it did not even hesitate.

There can be no ambiguity
in signals from the centre outwards
or the highest to the lowest point
but how does that apply here?

There must be some other type
of communication, the message
should draw you to itself and
be consumed.

In every few thousand collisions
there is one embrace,
a kind of prize at the bottom
someone finds, a hidden emblem
like an advantageous secret
meaningless to others;
a picture would sustain us
but the fading outline
is enough to let us identify it.

THE FIRST DREAM

The first dream in a new place
is always the most important.
Patches of ground show through &
that's how the surface is determined.
Danger waits in erosion
sand mixed with wind instead of water
the gradual reduction of all experience
through attention not neglect.
The ancient snowflake torture.

Tell me old woman do you still
see China when you dream?
Have the memories ground you to a powder
that you find in your clothes in the morning?
Is everything backwards when you study
the mirror—revering certain
references, deviating from others?

To relive is to revile it
even the old-fashioned thought of
its mechanism based on anomaly.
You concentrate until you bleed.

OPPORTUNITIES FOR REDEMPTION

Deliverance in the nick of time
is the highlight of my day,
the part I look forward to
and reflect on at night
during someone else's watch;
I imagine you are the same.

The rites of degustation
still mark the few of us who
were not ruined outright.
We are persons set apart: strangers
often remark that there's
something about the eyes,
they're not sure what exactly.

So we are brought to this place
by a twist of character
with its own vocabulary of
evasion and desire.
At this elevation we can hold
out almost indefinitely.

We monitor the ones down below,
tunnel out of view of those up above.
You think it's perfect, but do
not be misled.
Escape has not been brought to an end
but made permanent instead.
Flight is frozen.
There are no longer destinations
if there ever were.

VARIOUS SAVIOURS

They still tend towards invisibility
despite all the work they've done
revising their absence
for the sake of a basic pleasure
which afforded no other option than
a few irregular verbs like fossils
embedded in the language,
traces of an antique rebellion
of which no other record has survived.

(The red light on the police car
hiccups silently.)

One more tainted dawn and the
war's farewell to itself. That
is how it was written, such is how
old futurists must see it in their fantasies.
Every morning they review their dreams,
check the dream traffic, assess the direction,
looking for links and measuring fear
and comfort, seeking truth if evidence
won't do.

(One day a drunk returns from the dead
with all the latest rumours.)

This is not, they argue, some problem to be
solved in the jellied silence, but part
of the environment to be maintained from decay
(most of the damage unseen, underneath).
So let us begin that we may end.
I hear you asking: To what does
this sunrise pertain?
And distressed of all logic as you know me to be
I answer with a question of my own.

We've taken a vote you see.
As a saviour, frankly, you're next to worthless
if you can't discover a response.

(This inability to trust another person
—it is nature's defence against intrigue.)

THE DEAD KNOW BEST

even a good lawyer cannot kill the dead
—cummings

The signature inclines
towards the memory of another's
a reminder that gravity
leads only to the grave

one more precondition of
existence like it or not
a sign to fool the catechists
effective against all
their motherless bravado.

The past, most vegetant here,
nonetheless exploits our own
memories of it. Scars
caused by tears like
the track of a glacier that
bears down slowly in avoidance
of our wishes.

The dead know best:
lack of recent experience
makes them non-judgmental after a while.
And there are people here
from all walks of death
untinctured by our suspicions
the need to encrypt as well
as decipher
pausing midway from pawnshop
to madhouse somewhere in
the nether lands.

THE THIRTEEN USES OF SILENCE

Let's not make an issue of divinity
where the last of the idolaters is concerned.
For my taste, there is more than enough
immortality already, far beyond what
the circumstances warrant or
the amount recommended for defence.
It is simply that we need this music
to keep us warm, and it is carried on the books
as so much worship, unimportant in itself
but suggestive of a manner we are captive to.

Appearances travel, and which way does the ocean
trend this evening? When you have figured out
the sign, the direction, take me there please
without delay.

Quote the morning to me, fully and in context
(do not paraphrase). Quote it verbatim
and in the mothertongue. Quote the shapes hidden
in the geometric field after finding them by accident
make them public. We tame what we quote
and consume it by means of repetition.

When we have advertised our secrets, then what?
Shall we trade on the coincidence
or reaffirm the silence and its manner of address?
Silence is known by word of mouth;
it is a figure of speech you must imitate
before you can learn its tricks.
But do not allow it to reach a fever pitch
nor permit it to begin vibrating
spreading rumours of imminent noise.
The causes of silence are many. The uses
number thirteen in all.

CHINESE ANTHOLOGY

i.

A friend says she carries
an anthology of Chinese poetry
whenever she travels
but I travel lighter than she does
and substitute my own weak efforts
which I memorize along the way.
Poor retention prevents wordiness
& makes me stick to the point.

ii.

In the mountains this time of year
there are tracks on the frozen lake-beds
to prove with what urgency
and how little purpose
unselfconscious animals have wandered.
The truest line between two points
is often unpredictable,
the journeys themselves inevitable
even when least necessary.

So too here now.
Wherever I go I end up back on this
beach in the fog or drizzle
staring out at these tankers and freighters.
The same ones for months on end but
each night I return to find them
in some new arrangement
outlined with droopy strands of light
& I think how the dark water must
soothe their rusty old bellies.

iii.

I can only say
what is said in Li-Ki, the Book of Rites:

"Barring cogent reasons, a scholar is never
without his lute."
Of the culture you require, make however much
you can, bartering for the rest. Memory
is a type of appetite and you need
to make a habitat for habit to dwell in.
We have staked ours here, where the trick is
arranging the days
to be disadvantaged to the least extent
by events not totally in our control
and so support ourselves, living in the city
as though in the country
producing for need
tending one's garden so to speak
drinking from one's own cupped hands
watching the seasons change from prosperity to decay
seeking courage to await spring
and wisdom to see harvest as a process
not an act
nor even a strategy.
The place that comes of such suffering
was born in failure not success
which is the source of our want when we see
old proofs of other people's happiness.
Conduct yourself as though the world were still small
ignoring how the many now study the few
get beyond obscurity, anonymity
that's our advice
live as though distances were great
you'll go deeper that way
but remember the importance of ceremony
the book will always open at that page
if you teach and let yourself be taught.
Slightly more things are beginning than
are coming to an end:
the cross-fade of reference and echo.
The beauty of beauty is beauty against
such odds.

Beware of freelance holy men
and professional poets most of all
who darken the sky like an avian migration.

iv.

The thing returns to itself
and we go with it, to meet in reunion
having come with patient wisdom
to think the matter through.
Looking ahead to the armistice
keeps us from fear of the consequences.
We are here with our mops
and our brains to witness it.
The danger is always that the
present will lay down a carpet
of precedent for the future
to exploit
and that it will be merciless.
We do not rationalize, I assure you
but comb the transcripts for unexpected
gains (the losses were apparent
at the time).

v.

Ever since that dream in China
I don't know what the questions are.
Entire categories have shifted down
out of reach or simply vanished
an absence like ill fortune that feeds
on itself while the host
goes hungry.

I observe a vogue for censure
recast as private devotion
but have no idea what it means.
I suppose we must accept that some
events cause chaos while others don't.

May it help us to picture a rehearsal
for what we thought would happen
when the cruelty melts away:
a convenience for our imaging
like the Temple of the Garden of the Dead.

This mania for documentation must end.
Let it go forever in the kind of silence
that candour not caution impels.
For myself, I recall my father
who wore such brave clothes when he was young
and living by his wits
but in later years never found a place of
harmony to exercise his hard-won
ease with the vernacular.
The truth is: he never got over
the death of his father in 1938
when he was 23
and I've never got over his
when I was 17.
Tomb Sweeping Day is such a sentimental time.
As I have no children of my own
the duty thank god stops here.

vi.

One day we will not have to write in code.
One day the machinery of what we forget and what
we remember will no longer be so crucial.
One day we can stop killing time in the desert.
One day there will be room in the alcove.
One day it won't be such hard work to keep it simple.
One day chaos may not necessarily be a virtue.
One day she will be my rod and my staff.
One day there will be no more blood on the snow.
One day there will be no shock on the other side of the
door.
One day all will admire the lightness of her touch
and see that I was right.

One day you will not have to cross the borders to prove
        that they are real.
One day there will be no more conspiracy.
One day we will reach the statute of limitations.
Day of manumission, joyous time.

vii.

The deer are returning
in numbers you would have thought impossible.
It is not their hunger which lures them
from the woods, but ours. They see *us* starving
and *they* grow bold (not overconfident—bold).
They show no hubris, they do not curse
a losing streak, or pity themselves. They are realists
in how they have come to understand
that the clearing means safety as well as danger
that the one can't exist without the other
or would have no meaning if it did.

viii.

Those who knew him best
couldn't agree on his real name
or how old he was.
A speaker's preference said much
about the speaker, less about the
subject. A majority favoured
Nguyen Van Thanh
Nguyen Who Shall Be Victorious
an example of truth arrived at
democratically.
Then it was nineteen-eleven:
last year, a teacher without a diploma
this year, a student with no past.
His father grew rice you see
and studied and wrote the exams
but refused to speak the French printed
on the money they paid him with,

money he used to help the underground
for which his youngest son ran errands
no one suspecting a child
of complicity.
And when the boy was wise and ancient
he would sometimes startle visitors
by conversing in languages
they didn't know he knew.
Old men and their secrets.

ix.

Most nights I hear sirens
in the distance down below
of the sort that some people
stop noticing after a while
and others can only imagine.
This isn't meant as criticism.
After all, there are those who take
comfort from supposing that the sinner
must always return to the scene of the sin.

How many episodes were committed
in this hotel? It was either three or four.
I remember that man from the Bureau of Statistics
and think I see him on the fire escape
looking both ways down the alley as the
street-sweeper creeps past.
The circular brush is for grinding, not polishing.

Most of the ghosts are echoes.
They recall the silence accruing in the dark
as we've struggled to conclude
the unfinished conversations
left to us against our will.

Each evening the rain beats in
Every morning the maid makes up the room
so that nothing incriminating remains

beyond a few pencilled notes in the
margins of the Bible or another page missing
from the phone book.

Send down for some ice
While you're at it, send down for some fire.

x.

We shall meet once more
if you continue to remain
such a triumph over
everything foreseeable.
For my part, I intend
to become a hermit again.
No party will be complete
without my absence.
I shall practise amnesia
and encourage everyone to do
the same. I shall tell them:
Learn suspicion of spring days
for that is when the rectifiers
work hardest in their towers.
I want to write the kind of poems
that people write in prison
the kind you memorize a line a day
so you'll still know it when
the guards finally come to
pry the door open. Until then
I spend hours listening to the pages
printing out in the next room.
Fifty-four lines, a pause for breath.
Another fifty-four, pause again.
Whirling gears advance
the sheets pile up upon themselves
prefabricated leaves, mechanical autumn,
or blankets tied together for the escape
we've all been planning.

Underlining titles, the machine takes
on a deeper voice: a bailiff's
voice, dignified but self-important
announcing that court is now in session.
I leave the printer on all night.
Lying in the dark, I convince myself
that I've learned to tell when it's
typing your name
calling you to testify
in my defence.

DREAMING IN THE PLUPERFECT

The temptation can be apprehended if you keep
the river on your left. Please observe.
Spring floods discolour the low buildings. They are
stained around the bottom where a drunken tongue has licked
them, though one stands proud by a margin of two generations.
(I wonder who lived there, but of course you wouldn't know.)
The others are what was left when prosperity too receded.
These are questions travellers ask, lunging up the valley
with carefree dedication.

Events befall as usual. You cannot prevent them
from doing so. In the end, our dreams will be the only proof
that we were here, the warranty of efficient progress
and honest feeling. Newton's second law: objects in motion
tend to remain in motion if they have any say in the matter.
In the end, finally, it becomes a question of making salvation
look graceful.

I'm remembering that spot where the nun immolated herself.
I'm remembering the capital deserted. I'm remembering
the view through the one-way glass at the house in the
woods. I'm remembering the gravel crunching underfoot as we
waited for the expeditor. The speed is what stands out when
I have time for reflection. How lucky we were.

This is what must occur before the rest ensues:
morning's allusive gestures along the highway, we have
versioned it ourselves, we understand, we will stay you no more
with our sad story. We won't answer to the weather any longer
or whatever else may eventuate one day. Yet what happens next
is no less problematical. As we come into the world unwelcome
so must we try to glide unnoticed past fools and
sentimental tyrants.

It is autumn now as far as one could go in three days' drive.
Rain like footsteps following behind. We slow, it slows. We

speed up, it speeds up. All the leaves fall at once as though someone has pulled a rope. Soon snowflakes like asterisks will footnote the sky

thus:

* * * *

* * * * * *

MOTHER GODDESS

Just as the goddess rises dripping
from the lake like a woman on
an escalator whose topmost
step knows a moment of glory
on its way to
being reborn

so does the surf keep
slapping the beach like a
punctured tyre going round and round.

ART CRITICISM

Je suis ici pour faire des achats de dynamite.
—Blaise Cendrars

There are no guarantees
that anything will last
especially when you use
these inferior materials.

Thick chemical gesso
slides onto recycled canvas
one coat horizontal
the next vertical;
as soon as one dries,
another arrives to
contradict it.

I can't stand the silence.
My ears chafe waiting
for the tune of a catchy explosion.
I am the neighbourhood dynamiter
who never knows when opportunity
might strike. One must always
be alert and heavily armed
against success and its enemies.

This is how I am.
I have no patience
with craft for its own sake
not like the old
Chinese man standing
in his garden every morning
applying more red lacquer
to his coffin.

When the surface is hard
and shiny like a beetle
he will be venerated as only
the ancient dead can be.

I will be scattered over a wide area.
Parts of me may never be found.

AUTHOR'S NOTE

I had a normal adolescence, obsessed with Gandhi, Christ, Li Po, and Lee Harvey Oswald, sometimes to the point where it was no longer worth while trying to distinguish among them. It was in this context that I began writing poetry habitually, using it as a tool to see if I could register my experience in an accurate manner that might be accessible to others. "Deliver," included in this selection, is from a group written in 1965 when I'd just turned sixteen; it was one of the first poems I got published in a periodical. Others to be found here derive from *Our Man in Utopia* (Macmillan, 1971), *Achilles' Navel* (Press Porcépic, 1974), *Subroutines* (League of Canadian Poets, 1981), *Variorum* (Hounslow, 1985), *Rites of Alienation* (Quarry, 1988), *The Dreams of Ancient Peoples* (ECW, 1991), and *Chinese Anthology* (Reference West, 1992), as well from various broadsides, pamphlets, and chapbooks, some of them so obscure as to be almost covert. Conversely, the last couple of poems in this collection are ones printed here for the first time.

The arrangement, then, is generally chronological as well as more or less thematic. My poetry has certainly changed over the years, in matters of diction, density and orthography. Some of these shifts, however, have been the natural ricocheting that occurs when a period of using a short lyric form is followed by the desire for a longer line (or at least for longpoems). Such self-perpetuating alternation is common in poets today who have a love/hate relationship with their lyric selves. (The tug-of-war between Li Po, the spirited Taoist and dipsomaniac, and Tu Fu, the Confucian aesthete and antiquary obsessed with craft, continues yet. But it still does not preclude friendship between adherents of each, nor induce schizophrenia in those who are disciples of both.)

Given all that, I hope this *Selected Poems* will show that nonetheless I have been consistent. From the start, I was a political and religious poet (in that order), and so I have remained. This is the source of whatever puzzlement I may have engendered as well as of any organic sympathy I might have provoked along the way.

My thanks to all the publishers who printed these poems, or versions of them, earlier. Thanks also to Stephen Osborne for helping to rework the present manuscript and to Brian Lam for turning it into such a nice book.

Poems were little
flags we nailed to
the lefthand margin

No one saluted
no one surrendered
the wind blew past.

—Douglas Fetherling
Toronto/Vancouver, 1994